Animal Armor

Laura Marsh

NATIONAL
GEOGRAPHIC

Washington, D.C.

For Jane Strobel, a champion of children —L. F. M.

Design by YAY! Design

The publisher and author gratefully acknowledge the expert content review of this book by Sharon Glaeser, research associate of the Oregon Zoo, and the literacy review of this book by Mariam Jean Dreher, professor of reading education, University of Maryland, College Park.

Library of Congress Cataloging-in-Publication Data
Names: Marsh, Laura F., author. | National Geographic Society (U.S.)
Title: Animal armor / by Laura Marsh.
Description: Washington, D.C. : National Geographic Kids, [2018] | Series: National geographic readers | Audience: Ages 4-6. | Audience: Preschool, excluding K.
Identifiers: LCCN 2017015400 (print) | LCCN 2017020790 (ebook) | ISBN 9781426330360 (e-book) | ISBN 9781426330377 (e-book + audio) | ISBN 9781426330346 (pbk.) | ISBN 9781426330353 (hardcover)
Subjects: LCSH: Armored animals--Juvenile literature. | Animal defenses--Juvenile literature. | Adaptation (Biology)--Juvenile literature.
Classification: LCC QL940 (ebook) | LCC QL940 .M37 2018 (print) | DDC 591.47/7--dc23
LC record available at https://lccn.loc.gov/2017015400

Author's Note

The cover features the pangolin, one of the few mammals with scales. It is the most trafficked animal in the world, even though all eight species are protected by law. The title page shows a photo of a green tree python snake and the table of contents features a green June beetle.

Photo Credits

AL = Alamy Stock Photo, GI = Getty Images, NG = National Geographic Creative, SS = Shutterstock

Cover, George Steinmetz/GI; 1, Snowleopard1/GI; 3, gos-photodesign/SS; 4–5, Paul Souders/GI; 6, Clarence Holmes/AL; 7 (UP), Dr Morley Read/SS; 7 (LO), Sabena Jane Blackbird/AL; 8, Cigdem Sean Cooper/SS; 10, AfriPics.com/AL; 11, tratong/SS; 12, artcasta/SS; 13, zcw/SS; 14–15, Jak Wonderly; 16, Jurgen Freund/AL; 16 (INSET), Auscape/UIG via GI; 17, Bruno Guenard/GI; 18 (UP), W.E. Garrett/NG; 18 (CTR), Beth Swanson/SS; 18 (LO), Jak Wonderly; 19 (UP), Lori Skelton/SS; 19 (CTR), Comstock Images/GI; 19 (LO), Kamonrat/SS; 20, Paul van den Berg/SS; 21, stilllifephotographer/GI; 22, Michele Westmorland/GI; 23 (UP), Ben McRae/AL; 23 (LO), Fabian von Poser/AL; 24, Eric Isselée/SS; 25, Gerry Ellis/Minden Pictures; 26, Trevor Watchous/EyeEm/GI; 27 (UP), Christian Ziegler/NG; 27 (LO), scubaluna/SS; 28–29, NH/SS; 28, Juan Manuel Borrero/Nature Picture Library; 29, NatalieJean/SS; 30 (LE), Michael Nichols/NG; 30 (RT), Ryan M. Bolton/SS; 31 (UP LE), Rudmer Zwerver/SS; 31 (UP RT), Fedor Selivanov/SS; 31 (LO LE), Rich Carey/SS; 31 (LO RT), Marc Parsons/SS; 32 (UP LE), Peter Titmuss/SS; 32 (UP RT), Paul Souders/GI; 32 (LO LE), Paul van den Berg/SS; 32 (LO RT), Cigdem Sean Cooper/SS; top border, Fecundap stock/SS; vocabulary box art, Serg001/SS

National Geographic supports K–12 educators with ELA Common Core Resources. Visit natgeoed.org/commoncore for more information.

Printed in the United States of America
17/WOR/1

Table of Contents

A Cover of Armor

These lions are hungry. They want to eat this porcupine. But they know to beware! The porcupine has body armor.

Some animals have spines. Others have hard shells. And some have thick, bumpy skin. Body armor helps keep animals safe.

Sharp Spines

Would you want to touch these animals? Probably not.

Each spine is sharp and pointy. Spines tell a predator (PRED-uh-tur) to back off. Sharp spines are painful.

saddleback moth caterpillar

spiny bush cricket

spiny orb weaver

Cover Word

PREDATOR:
An animal that hunts and eats other animals

lionfish

Lots of animals have spines. A lionfish has special ones. These spines have venom. If a predator tries to eat the lionfish, venom will enter the predator's skin.

Cover Word

VENOM: A liquid some animals make that kills or harms other animals

Stay away from a
porcupine!

Its sharp spines are
called quills. They
shake and rattle
when danger is near.
The quills can stick
into an enemy.
Ouch!

These quills* from an
Old World porcupine
have fallen out.

*not life-size

Old World porcupine

11

Strong Shells

When a snail moves, most of its soft body is outside its shell.

Q What is the strongest animal?

A A snail! It carries its house on its back.

A shell is another kind of armor. It protects an animal's soft body.

Snails and clams can pull their bodies inside their shells. They can't move quickly, but they can hide!

These snails have pulled their bodies all the way into their shells.

Many turtles can do this, too.
They pull their legs and head inside.

Western pond turtle

A turtle has an upper shell and a lower shell. Both shells are hard, and they grow with the turtle. The turtle's body is attached to the shell.

red-eared slider turtle

Did you know? A turtle can feel when its shell is touched.

Other animals have a hard
covering over their whole body—
even their legs.

Christmas Island red crabs

old shell

This kind of shell doesn't grow. When the animal grows, its shell gets too small. The animal sheds the old shell. Then it makes a new one. This is called molting.

damselfly

A damselfly sheds its old shell.

6 COOL FACTS About Animal Armor

1

Many people think porcupines "shoot" their quills. They don't. Some porcupines have quills that come off when a predator touches them.

A pufferfish has spines that lie flat. But it can swallow water to make its spines stick out.

2

3

Many animals with body armor move slowly. The armor protects them when they can't get away from predators.

4 an eagle's toes

All birds have scales— on their toes!

A giant clam can be four feet long and weigh as much as three adult men (up to 500 pounds).

5

6

A hedgehog has spines on its head and back. When it rolls into a ball, its soft face and belly stay safe from predators.

Super Scales

marine iguana

kingsnake

When you think about reptiles, do you think of scales?

Scales are small, hard plates on the skin. Lizards, crocodiles, turtles, and snakes have them. Scales protect their skin.

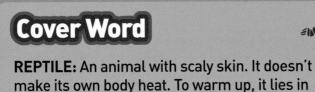

Cover Word

REPTILE: An animal with scaly skin. It doesn't make its own body heat. To warm up, it lies in the sun. To cool down, it lies in the shade.

white grunt fish

Reptiles aren't the only animals with scales. Fish and a few mammals have them, too.

pangolin

The pangolin (PAN-go-lin) is a mammal with thick, sharp scales. It can roll into a ball. This makes it hard for predators to eat.

Cover Word

MAMMAL: An animal that feeds its babies milk. It can keep its body temperature the same at all times.

A pangolin rolls into a ball for protection.

23

Scales don't only make the skin tough (TUFF). They also keep an animal from drying out.

frilled lizard

thorny dragon

In hot areas, water is hard to find.
Animals with scales need less
water to live.

green crested lizard

leaf chameleon

Scales have color. They form patterns, too. This helps an animal hide from its enemies. Can you find the animals hiding here?

great rockfish

Armor All Around

Lots of animals have body armor that helps keep them safe. If you could have armor, what kind would you choose?

pearl cichlid

sea urchin

rhinoceros beetle

What in the World?

These pictures show up-close views of animals with body armor. Use the hints to figure out what's in the pictures. Answers are on page 31.

1

HINT: A porcupine rattles these when danger is near.

2

HINT: To shed a shell and grow a new one

Word Bank

turtle   scales   hedgehog   molt   quills   lionfish

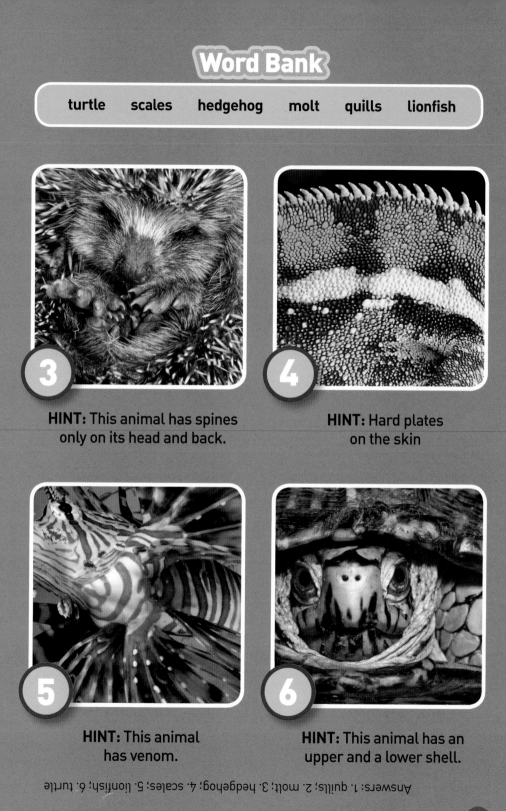

3

HINT: This animal has spines only on its head and back.

4

HINT: Hard plates on the skin

5

HINT: This animal has venom.

6

HINT: This animal has an upper and a lower shell.

Answers: 1. quills; 2. molt; 3. hedgehog; 4. scales; 5. lionfish; 6. turtle

MAMMAL: An animal that feeds its babies milk. It can keep its body temperature the same at all times.

PREDATOR: An animal that hunts and eats other animals

REPTILE: An animal with scaly skin. It doesn't make its own body heat. To warm up, it lies in the sun. To cool down, it lies in the shade.

VENOM: A liquid some animals make that kills or harms other animals